Profitable Rentals That Produce Mailbox Money

By Todd Swanson and Dan Williams

San Diego, CA

Copyright © MMXXIV by Todd Swanson and Dan Williams.

All rights reserved. No part of this publication may be reproduced or transmitted in any form or by any means electronic or mechanical, including photocopy, recording, or any information storage and retrieval system now know or to be invented, without permission in writing from the publisher, except by a reviewer who wishes to quote brief passages in connection with a review written for inclusion in a magazine, newspaper, or broadcast.

Visit our Web site at **www.NotSoGoldenCA.com** for more information on how to profitably invest in rental properties.

Published in the United States of America by Todd Swanson and Dan Williams.

7290 Navajo Road Suite 104
San Diego, CA 92119

Disclaimer: Investing in financial markets involves risk. Past performance is not indicative of future results. Any investment decision should be made based on individual risk tolerance, financial situation, and investment objectives. It's important to carefully consider all information and seek advice from a qualified professional before making any investment decisions. No guarantee is made regarding the accuracy or completeness of the information provided, and no responsibility is assumed for any financial losses incurred as a result of using this information. All investments carry inherent risks, and investors should be prepared to bear the possibility of loss. The content provided is for informational purposes only and should not be construed as investment advice or a recommendation to buy, sell, or hold any securities or financial products.

Table of Contents

Introduction 7

Mailbox Money 9

Real Estate Has An Unfair Advantage 19

Cash Flow Is King 25

Buy Right And The Market Doesn't Matter 33

The Place To Invest Is The Mid-west 41

Three Is Better Than One 49

The Magic Of Ten Thirty One 53

What Life Will Be Like For You 59

Glossary 65

Appendix 1 – Problematic Ways Of Measuring The Success (Or Potential Success) Of A Rental Property .. 69

Appendix 2 – Financing Terms For Single-Family Rental Property Loans 71

About the Authors 75

    Todd Swanson 77

    Dan Williams 79

Exclusive Bonuses 81

Introduction

I met Todd back in 2009 at a private event for select members of a coaching group. In our conversations we discovered a common interest beyond the mortgage business. We were (and still are) driven by a desire to assist others with achieving financial freedom and independence through real estate investing. Shortly after that private event we began collaborating on business systems to create a smoother process for our clients. As a result of our close working relationship, both of us became better; as the saying goes, "iron sharpens iron."

An example of this is the course that we developed for real estate agents on investment property analysis. The California Department of Real Estate approved it as continuing education. We taught that class together many times. Our collaboration has enabled us to help over 2000 families with their home mortgages and investment property financing.

As lifelong learners, we have worked diligently over the years to upgrade our skill sets thru education and training with industry leaders, often in one-on-one coaching, and thru certifications such as the Certified Liability Advisor™.

"Real estate investing, even on a very small scale, remains a tried-and-true means of building an individual's cash flow and wealth." – Robert Kiyosaki

All of this is driven by our desire to ensure we are providing the value we believe our clients deserve; to aid you in decreasing your risk and maximize your real estate investment returns. You will see this throughout this book and in our YouTube videos and classes that we teach.

Personally, I'm excited for you to read this book, because Todd has taken his personal experience with real estate investing and has shared those hard-earned lessons in such an easy-to-read and engaging manner. His story will enable you to increase your wealth and freedom. I know you will enjoy reading this amazing story.

Daniel Williams

"Real estate investing, even on a very small scale, remains a tried-and-true means of building an individual's cash flow and wealth." – Robert Kiyosaki

Chapter 1

Mailbox Money

"Money is a terrible master but an excellent servant."
P.T. Barnum

Real estate has fascinated me since I was a teenager. My friend's father was a real estate agent, property flipper and home builder. Meanwhile, both of my parents worked in salaried government jobs.

My parents had security.

My friend's father had freedom.

The difference intrigued me and still does. What I found most interesting about real estate was the many ways that wealth can be created through it.

"Real estate investing, even on a very small scale, remains a tried-and-true means of building an individual's cash flow and wealth." – Robert Kiyosaki

One method is to buy single family homes as long-term rentals. The subject of this book is how to do that profitably (maybe it would be better to say 'correctly').

My goal in this book is to share the nuts and bolts of how to put together a portfolio of single-family rental homes that produce high cash flow or what we like to call mailbox money – that's consistent rising income with tax benefits that come from a tangible asset that we all understand and that increases in value over time.

That's mailbox money.

We live in a cash flow world. Think back to when you last rented, do you think your landlord had a smile on his face when he cashed your rent check? *There's a good chance, right?*

Our bills are typically due monthly, so <u>shouldn't our investments pay us the same way?</u>

"Real estate investing, even on a very small scale, remains a tried-and-true means of building an individual's cash flow and wealth." – Robert Kiyosaki

Ask yourself this, how would my life be different if my investments were sending me a consistent pay check? *Wouldn't that give you peace of mind?*

A big part of the retirement problem in America is that we lock up our money for decades in confusing products that most of us don't understand and that often benefit Wall Street more than Main Street.

Would you agree that most Americans have no idea what their retirement income is going to be?

As a result, most American's don't save enough and they don't grow their investments fast enough, all because they don't understand retirement well enough. I want to change retirement for the people in my life; for the people that my business comes in contact with.

"Real estate investing, even on a very small scale, remains a tried-and-true means of building an individual's cash flow and wealth." – Robert Kiyosaki

We've all been on the wrong side of Mailbox Money (we call them bills) at one time in our lives. My goal is to change that. To help you diversify out of Wall Street, to understand your investments, to create an alternate stream of income and to create a legacy.

At this point it is necessary to say that I recommend that real estate investors have a financial advisor. My earlier statement might make it appear otherwise, but that is absolutely not the case. The fact is that a good financial advisor will assist you with filling in the gaps in your financial protections. They will act as your guide in the maze of confusing, but often necessary Wall Street products – many of which are essential to have a solid foundation.

A real estate investor who has nothing saved outside of his rentals is a higher risk than an investor who has money saved in retirement accounts. This difference is dramatically displayed in the kinds of loans and interest rates available to each investor. As a Mortgage Planner, I always encourage my clients to hire a great financial advisor. So much so, that I am often the one who introduced them to their advisor.

"Real estate investing, even on a very small scale, remains a tried-and-true means of building an individual's cash flow and wealth." – Robert Kiyosaki

Now, back to the topic of Mailbox Money, here's an example:

This house is on Caroline drive in Horn Lake, MS. I paid $151,000 for it in February of 2022, just before interest rates took off. It rents for $1295. We put 20% down and took out a crazy 40-year fixed rate mortgage at 3.99% with the option to pay interest only for the first 10 years. That makes my mortgage payment including taxes and insurance, just $528 per month!

Here's the kicker, that's not even the best cash flow market.

There are others that produce even higher cash flow.

"Real estate investing, even on a very small scale, remains a tried-and-true means of building an individual's cash flow and wealth." – Robert Kiyosaki

You may have watched the Netflix show Chef's Table Pizza. Chris Bianco, standing next to me is the focus of episode 1. If you haven't seen the show, go check it out. I really enjoyed his story. He has been called the best pizza chef in the world by Martha Stewart and many others.

Chris was paid to speak to a group called Metrix Mastermind. It's a coaching organization that only works with the top real estate agents in the country (and a few top loan officers like me). This event was by invitation only and the membership is crazy expensive, but as a result, they have some amazing content and awesome guest speakers. And my production as a Mortgage Planner and experience as an investor are what got me into that room.

In the last 5 years, we have helped over 160 investors with financing their rental properties – almost all single-family houses.

"Real estate investing, even on a very small scale, remains a tried-and-true means of building an individual's cash flow and wealth." – Robert Kiyosaki

Personally, I purchased my first rental property 24 years ago. Along the way, I've had some wins, some losses, and I've learned a few lessons. Benjamin Franklin wrote that there are two types of experience: earned and borrowed and that the latter is far cheaper. My goal in this book is to impart to you the most important lessons from that experience.

At the end of this book - with your permission - I'm going to share an opportunity that you may find incredibly valuable or not. That's up to you. I'm not going do a commercial in these pages. This is pure awesome content based on 22 years of investing experience. At the end, I'm going to share how you can get some more help on this topic if you choose. *Fair enough?*

In the meantime, there are a going to be a few things that we have to deal with if you are going to be successful; legitimate concerns.

The first is time. You may already be thinking that you can't afford to learn this by trial and error and you just don't have the time to study this. To me, this is the biggest challenge of all. I understand that you find yourself most likely in a situation today

---

"Real estate investing, even on a very small scale, remains a tried-and-true means of building an individual's cash flow and wealth." – Robert Kiyosaki

where time is at a premium. The fact is the less time you have, the more you'll love the approach that I will share with you today.

You may also have some confusion about real estate investing. Where do I start? How will it all work? You know, finding a property, screening a tenant, dealing with maintenance, etc. I get it. If it were clear to you already, you would already be doing it. But what one man can learn, so can another and you aren't going to be on this journey alone.

Another concern you may be thinking is, "What if I screw this up? What if I make a mistake?" Here's a newsflash – you will, but we are going to put a system in place that limits the downside while maintaining the upside. We are going to limit risk.

Today, you'll discover some tools and tricks to mitigate the big risks, so that any mistakes are small change. In other words, you'll learn all the way the bank.

Given all the weird stuff that has gone on in the economy the last few years, you may be thinking, is this the right time? Did I miss the boat? Should I wait for a better time? I get it, because before I put all of the pieces of this puzzle together, I wondered

---

"Real estate investing, even on a very small scale, remains a tried-and-true means of building an individual's cash flow and wealth." – Robert Kiyosaki

that as well. As you read this book, you'll discover the way to know exactly when to invest and under what criteria to ensure that you've made a profitable investment.

Let's say I had a time machine and I let you take it for a spin. You hopped in and it brought you to the exact point where you have mastered everything I laid out in this book. You have the ability to help the people you care about, because you are in a much better financial position. You're more confident in your ability to create and grow wealth than ever before.

What are you going to do now that you have all this extra time on your hands, because you've replaced your income with mailbox money; steady passive income from your rentals that you receive in your mailbox every month?

"Real estate investing, even on a very small scale, remains a tried-and-true means of building an individual's cash flow and wealth." – Robert Kiyosaki

You could play more golf. True. But what are the higher pursuits that you've always wanted to go after, yet in the past seemed like wishful thinking?

I bet they are good things. Well, actually let me take that back. I bet they are _great_ things. More time with your loved ones. Time to volunteer at your church or a charity that matters to you. Jim Rohn expressed it well when he said, "Set a goal not simply for attainment of the goal, but for what it makes of you to achieve it."

In this book we are going to discuss the means, but the end is who it makes you as a person. And that is exciting to me! Because as far as I'm concerned, your journey to get there starts now!

So we are going to talk about:
- Why real estate has an unfair advantage when compared to other investments.
- The one element of real estate investing that matters more than any other.
- The right strategies to mitigate risk in your investment.
- Where to find the best properties

"Real estate investing, even on a very small scale, remains a tried-and-true means of building an individual's cash flow and wealth." – Robert Kiyosaki

Chapter 2

Real Estate Has An Unfair Advantage

"Buy land, they're not making it anymore."
Mark Twain

Let's start with the fact that Real Estate has an unfair advantage. There are four benefits that real estate investing has that other investments only have some of. The four benefits are appreciation, cash flow, tax advantages, and leverage.

Let's look at the first one - appreciation. Growth stocks are purchased on speculation that they will rise in price over time enabling the investor to sell at a higher price for a profit. Real estate 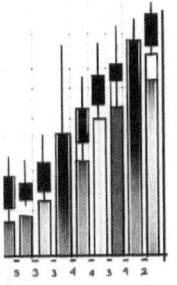  provides this same benefit and has averaged 4% annual appreciation since the end of World War II. Here's how to put a 4% rate of appreciation into perspective. *Your property value will*

"Real estate investing, even on a very small scale, remains a tried-and-true means of building an individual's cash flow and wealth." - Robert Kiyosaki

double every 18 years. Thus a $151,000 rental house will be worth $302,000 in 18 years.

The second benefit is cash flow. Bonds and rental properties produce cash flow to the investor. With regard to rental property cash flow, I am referring to money left over from the rents after all expenses and set-asides have been taken out, including amortization on the loan.

Now, going back to bonds, with very few exceptions, the bond income is fixed and doesn't change during the life of the bond. However, rental income does increase over time and since it tracks real estate values (with a little bit of lag) it has also increased at 4% annually since the end of World War II. Thus, your $1295 per month in rent will be $2600 per month in 18 years. Meanwhile, your mortgage payment has remained the same. Bonds don't do that. Isn't it already starting to get unfair?

Now this is where it gets really unfair. Real Estate has tax advantages that stocks and bonds only wish they had. Some bonds produce tax free income and stocks can be owned in a

"Real estate investing, even on a very small scale, remains a tried-and-true means of building an individual's cash flow and wealth." – Robert Kiyosaki

ROTH IRA, thus making their growth tax free, but only real estate has the option to produce tax deductions that have the ability to not only make your cash flow tax free, but can also be used as a tax deduction against other income. Think about having more take home pay from your job, because you are a real estate investor.

Pretty cool, right?

Finally, we come to leverage. This is where it truly becomes flat-out, completely, no-holds barred, unfair. No other investment can employ the sheer amount of leverage that real estate can. Leverage, by the way, is borrowed money used to purchase the investment. Stocks and Bonds are only allowed to be leverage up to 50%, but real estate can be leveraged up to 100% of its value. More than that, the financing that you can employ is fixed and stable with a long-term payment structure (such as a 30-year fixed rate mortgage). Once you have it in place your loan is no longer subject to market forces. If the cost of the money you borrowed is less than the investment produces, then the leverage magnifies your return.

"Real estate investing, even on a very small scale, remains a tried-and-true means of building an individual's cash flow and wealth." – Robert Kiyosaki

I'll say that again, if the interest rate on your loan is lower than the return your investment produces, then your loan increases your rate of return. Let's look at an example:

Property value	Down payment	Loan	Net Income	rate of return
$400,000	$400,000	$0	$28,000	7%
A $400,000 property purchased all in cash that produces $28,000 in net income is providing a 7% cash-on-cash return				
$400,000	$100,000	$300,000	$10,000	10%
If the $400k equity was used to purchase 4 properties				
$1,600,000	$400,000	$1,200,000	$40,000	10%

- A $400,000 property purchased all in cash that produces $28,000 in net income is providing a 7% cash-on-cash return
- Assuming a 6% interest rate on the $300,000 loan, the rate of return rises to 10%.
- By only putting $100,000 down, the investor has the option to purchase 3 more properties, thus producing $40,000 in net income.
- Add in 4% appreciation on the four properties and you have another 16% paper gain.
- If you also have a tax deduction against your earned income… to quote Donnie Brasco, "fuhgetaboutit!"

"Real estate investing, even on a very small scale, remains a tried-and-true means of building an individual's cash flow and wealth." – Robert Kiyosaki

Are you starting see just how awesome real estate investing can be when done right?

So, Real Estate has an unfair advantage, because it can appreciate, because it produces cash flow that can also rise over time. It has an unfair advantage, because it offers tax advantages. And, finally, Real estate has an unfair advantage, because it can be leveraged at a higher rate than any other investment and leverage magnifies returns.

"Real estate investing, even on a very small scale, remains a tried-and-true means of building an individual's cash flow and wealth." – Robert Kiyosaki

Chapter 3

Cash Flow Is King

"The three most dreaded words in the English language are 'negative cash flow'."
David Tang

Now we are going to focus on the one element of real estate investing that matters more than any other: Cash flow. Between cash flow, appreciation, and the tax benefits that come with real estate investing, cash flow is king.

An investment property that produces cash flow is like a hen that consistently lays eggs – it's dependable. Appreciation is like a pig; you don't get a meal until you slaughter it. While appreciation creates equity, you can't spend it. You have to first convert the equity into cash. You have to sell the property or do a cash out refinance, but that's like ending up with a 3-legged pig. You kill your cash flow

"Real estate investing, even on a very small scale, remains a tried-and-true means of building an individual's cash flow and wealth." – Robert Kiyosaki

in order to eat the ham. As we talk about why cash flow is king, we are going to discuss the problems with investing primarily for appreciation, which are a problem of compounding, lower cash flow, volatility, and the four threats to equity.

So, the first problem of investing for appreciation is the problem of compounding. Albert Einstein famously said that compound interest is the most powerful force in the universe. You can't reinvest your appreciation unless you slaughter the pig. Thus, you cannot compound equity. However, you can compound cash flow. <u>Wall Street understands this, but Main Street typically doesn't.</u>

You can reinvest your cash flow into other investments; your eggs can produce more hens. Your cash flow can become the down payment for your next property. Isn't that an exciting thought?

Significantly lower cash flow is the next problem with investing for appreciation. The markets that produce higher appreciation also produce less rent as a percentage of the price.

26

"Real estate investing, even on a very small scale, remains a tried-and-true means of building an individual's cash flow and wealth." – Robert Kiyosaki

For example, a $1mil home here in San Diego owned free and clear would be around $5000/mo. in rent. For that same amount of equity, other markets would produce $10,000/mo.

You may recall the character from the Popeye cartoons, who had the line, "I will gladly pay you Tuesday for a hamburger today." In essence, an investor provides the hamburger upfront and has to hope to get paid back at some Tuesday in the future. Not only do they have the opportunity cost of half the rent, they are also speculating that one of the four threats to cash flow won't affect them. In a bit I will cover what the Four threats to cash flow are and how to mitigate them. But, think about this, the appreciation market starts out $5000 per month behind the cash flow markets. You are going to need to have a significantly higher rate of appreciation to make up that ground. Never mind the fact that cash in hand beats profits on paper. All things being equal, wouldn't you want more rent rather than less?

"Real estate investing, even on a very small scale, remains a tried-and-true means of building an individual's cash flow and wealth." – Robert Kiyosaki

Now at this point, the response I often hear from investors who already own a positive cash flow rental property in Southern California, is that the cash flow compared to their original investment is really good, so why mess with a good thing.

The problem is your Return-on-Equity (your annual profits divided by the equity in the property). Let's assume an original purchase price ten years ago was $500,000 with a 10% down payment. If you are bringing in $500 per month spendable cash flow ($6000 per year), then your Cash-on-Cash return (the annual cash flow divided by the cash invested) seems pretty good; in this example it is a 12% cash on cash return.

That positive cash flow no doubt feels good, but it misses the much larger cash flow your equity could be producing. If the property value is now $650,000, then your equity in the property is over $200,000. That makes the return on equity just 3%...not so exciting. Imagine what the return on equity would be if your rent was double the amount that it is today.

That's an exciting thought isn't it?

"Real estate investing, even on a very small scale, remains a tried-and-true means of building an individual's cash flow and wealth." – Robert Kiyosaki

The third problem of investing for appreciation is volatility. They rise the fastest in good times and are first to fall in bad times. They can depreciate and a Bear market can wipe out your profits.

That's kind of like spending money to fatten up the pig, hoping to sell it for a large profit only to have a bear break into the pen and eat the pig.

Rents don't have this problem. Rents are sticky. They lag behind the rise in housing prices and they rarely decline. Barring something like Hurricane Katrina blowing thru New Orleans and causing the city to empty out, the worst case with rents typically is that they just flatten out for a period of time. Your hens are safe in the hen house. Right?

Now let's compare appreciation markets against cash flow markets to see how they each handle the four threats to equity. The first is a lawsuit, which requires cash to fight and cash to pay

"Real estate investing, even on a very small scale, remains a tried-and-true means of building an individual's cash flow and wealth." – Robert Kiyosaki

a judgement. Second is Foreclosure, which results from an inability to make the payment. Third is depreciation (which we already talked about), and, the last is appreciation. That may surprise you, but it is the catalyst for other things, such as an increase in property taxes or the need to raise replacement cost coverage on an insurance policy.

Sometimes it can even be the catalyst for a lawsuit; someone with a large amount equity can become target. All four of those threats (lawsuits, foreclosure, depreciation, and appreciation) can be mitigated via cash flow, but not with equity. For example, a property that cash flows in a depreciating market is throwing off profits despite the decline in values.

The four threats to equity are like being caught in a rainstorm. If you have cash flow you can buy an umbrella, but you can't with appreciation. Are you starting to see that investing primarily for cash flow makes more sense than

---

"Real estate investing, even on a very small scale, remains a tried-and-true means of building an individual's cash flow and wealth." – Robert Kiyosaki

investing primarily for appreciation?

So, here's what we've covered: investing for appreciation is like raising a pig, because you can't spend appreciation and you can't compound it. To do either one you have to slaughter the pig to convert the equity to cash. Also, you receive far less in rent, which is like giving away a hamburger today hoping to get paid on Tuesday. Appreciation markets are far more volatile; the bear could kill the pig. And finally, when the threats to equity 'rainstorm' catches you outside, you can buy an umbrella with cash flow, but not with appreciation. That's why Cash flow is King.

It's the Goose that lays the golden eggs. Wouldn't it be nice if more money showed up in your life more often? You can see that investing for Cash flow instead of appreciation does that, can't you? It produces mailbox money.

"Real estate investing, even on a very small scale, remains a tried-and-true means of building an individual's cash flow and wealth." – Robert Kiyosaki

Chapter 4

Buy Right And The Market Doesn't Matter

"The major fortunes in America have been made in land."
John D. Rockefeller

At this point we've talked about the fact that real estate has an unfair advantage and that cash flow is king.

Now let's move to the right strategy to mitigate risk in your investment, which is buy right and the market doesn't matter.

The better you are at picking the right investment, the worse you can be at everything else.

In other words, if your ship is sound, the rising and falling of the tides won't affect it. With real estate investing, there are four criteria to mitigating market risk: buy the right community, buy the right inspections, buy the right financing, and buy the

---

"Real estate investing, even on a very small scale, remains a tried-and-true means of building an individual's cash flow and wealth." – Robert Kiyosaki

right management. If you do those four things, you will buy right and the market won't matter.

Let's start with buying the right community. We want to build a house on rock, not on sand. The community is the foundation for the investment. Research the metropolitan area, and the communities within that metro area, because every metro area has sweet spots for investing – stable areas where high quality tenants want to live, but that isn't so expensive that they are priced out.

An area that is gentrifying is a positive sign. Imagine you've just toured a small 3-bedroom, 1-bath home with your real estate agent. It's an older home in an older neighborhood, but it has been tastefully remodeled. Gone is the old 1960s bathroom and it's been replaced with a fully tiled shower, new vanity, new tile flooring. In short, the bathroom looks great. The Kitchen has had the same

---

"Real estate investing, even on a very small scale, remains a tried-and-true means of building an individual's cash flow and wealth." – Robert Kiyosaki

treatment done it. In fact, the whole house has been freshened up and appears to be in really good shape. As you walk out of house to head back to your car, you notice the neighborhood is all single-story homes except for a couple of homes just three doors down. Those two homes look like they were recently built and they are two stories, so you ask your Realtor. She proceeds to tell you that those two lots previously contained homes like the one you just looked at. A developer recently came in, tore them down, and put those two houses, which are each 5 bedrooms 3 baths. Unless that developer is a complete fool, you've just found a fantastic indicator that this is the right kind of community. The area is gentrifying and will perform well as a buy and hold investment.

Do you agree that buying the right community is building your house, your investment portfolio, on a foundation of rock? It just makes sense, doesn't it?

The second criteria to buy right and ensure that the market doesn't matter, is to buy the right inspections. We want to go into this with our eyes wide open, not with a blind fold. The best way to accomplish this is to pay

"Real estate investing, even on a very small scale, remains a tried-and-true means of building an individual's cash flow and wealth." – Robert Kiyosaki

experts to look in every nook and cranny of the prospective investment and then provide you with a detailed report with pictures and notes, so that you have a full understanding of the condition of the home.

This is more than just a standard home inspection, although a home inspection is often the jumping off point. Anything that comes up in the inspection we can bring in subject matter experts to give us their detailed reports and cost estimates for repair or replacement, because you will see it better with their eyes than you would ever see it with your own. Maybe the home inspection highlights the age of the water heater and the HVAC, so you call in a plumbing, heating, and air company and get their professional opinion on the condition of the system. In this case they recommend replacing the water heater and they give you a cost estimate for doing it. A quick check of vendors in the area tells you that their bid is reasonable and it's within the budget you set for getting home rent ready, so you make plans to do that after the close. Also, they tell you the HVAC is in good working order and should continue to be reliable for several more years, so you check that off you list.

Nobody likes surprises.

Can you see how buying the right inspections prevents those surprises? It takes the blind fold off, doesn't it? We *go into the investment with our eyes wide open.*

The third (of the four) criteria for buying right is buy the right financing. There's a saying that when the person next to you loses money, it's a recession, but when you lose money, it's a depression. To which I would add, if the person next to you losing money is your spouse, then it's an argument. Losing money on an investment – it would be fair to call that a financial crisis, wouldn't it? Buying the right financing avoids your own personal financial crisis.

A decade ago, people who thought they were investing were in fact gambling. They bought properties that wouldn't cash flow if they had a fixed rate mortgage, so they took out variable rate mortgages often with prepayment penalties and teaser rates, and sometimes even a balloon payment – this a requirement to pay off the mortgage early in a lump sum.

"Real estate investing, even on a very small scale, remains a tried-and-true means of building an individual's cash flow and wealth." - Robert Kiyosaki

Thus, they foolishly bet that either rents would increase fast enough to make up for the future interest rate increase and that the home value would climb enough to make up for the loses. In essence, they were betting that a bigger fool would come along to buy the home from them.

Buy the right financing means take out a long term 30-year fixed rate mortgage that has a stable payment that will never change, has no balloon, requires you to have additional savings as a safety net – they don't want you "all in" – that's gambling. So, you buy a home with the right financing and it cash flows upfront. Then the magic happens…rents increase over time, but your mortgage payment stays the same. A couple of years down the line and you are cashing a bigger and bigger check. Buy the right financing and you will avoid a financial crisis. Agreed?

The fourth and last criteria for buying right is buy the right management. A good property manager is like a bouncer at a night club; they are only going to let the right people in. The most obvious "right people" are the

"Real estate investing, even on a very small scale, remains a tried-and-true means of building an individual's cash flow and wealth." – Robert Kiyosaki

tenants, but it extends beyond that to service people and their own employees. When repairs need to be made, we want them sending in the right technicians – individuals who will act with honesty and integrity, who are skilled at their trade, and will do the job right. When their employees show the property or do the turnover with an out-going tenant, we want them to be thorough, honest, and ethical; be fair with the tenant, but protect our interests.

It's like this, you get your monthly check and notice that your usual $5200 is check is a little bit lower that month, just over $5000. So you peruse the monthly statement and see a note that they replaced the compressor on the HVAC system. You remember that when you bought the home you paid for an HVAC inspection and that guy had said it would need to be replaced in the next couple of years, so it's not a surprise. But then the next thought occurs to you – "I didn't pay for it. My tenant did…and I still have a positive cash flow!" In short, a good property manager, like a good bouncer, is going to protect your investment. Makes sense, right?

To review, you buy right if you build your house on rock, not on sand by doing your due diligence on the right community.

"Real estate investing, even on a very small scale, remains a tried-and-true means of building an individual's cash flow and wealth." – Robert Kiyosaki

You buy right if you go into the investment with your eyes wide open, you take the blind fold off by doing all the right inspections. You buy right by getting the right financing, which avoids gambling – a potential financial crisis. You buy right if your property manager, like a good bouncer, only lets in the right people. Therefore, if your ship is sound, the rising and falling of the tides doesn't matter.

I thought of using a storm analogy – as in 'can weather a storm' – but that isn't the right analogy, because if you buy right… then there is no storm. You will just have the rising and falling of the tides. If we follow the four steps to buy right, then we don't have to fear screwing this up do we? With these four steps, can you see that buying right ensures mailbox money?

Chapter 5

The Place To Invest Is The Mid-west

"Never take your eyes off the cash flow because it's the lifeblood of the business."
Sir Richard Branson

Okay, so at this point we have talked about the fact that real estate has an unfair advantage, that cash flow is king, and that if we buy right the market doesn't matter. Now let's talk about where to find the best properties. The place to invest is the mid-west (and the broader "heartland").

In this section we are going to talk about three things: first, the mid-west cash flow difference, second, how to safely invest from a distance, then we will review how to mitigate the four threats to cash flow.

So first, the mid-west cash flow difference versus buying a rental property in California is like the difference between a fancy restaurant and a buffet. In the fancy restaurant, you pay a lot and

you leave hungry. You have to go get a cheeseburger afterwards. You aren't going to have cash flow. And that's like buying a rental in California.

Worse than that, you might even have to add money to the investment account when you get hit by one of the four threats to cash flow. I'm going to cover those in a minute. But first, think about eating at a buffet restaurant; you get a lot more food for a much lower price, that's what investing in the mid-west is like. In this analogy, the food is the cash flow. With that in mind, imagine going to the buffet restaurant and eating your fill, then packing three to go boxes. That's like budgeting for vacancy (those periods when you don't have a tenant), budgeting for maintenance (something like a stopped-up toilet), and budgeting for capital expenditures (think roof replacement).

Thus, we not only want the property to produce mailbox money – money we can spend or reinvest, but don't we also want it to produce reserves for vacancy, maintenance, and capital expenditures? That's just a good business practice, isn't it?

"Real estate investing, even on a very small scale, remains a tried-and-true means of building an individual's cash flow and wealth." – Robert Kiyosaki

In the earlier example, I mentioned that if you owned a million-dollar home here in San Diego, at the time of this writing, the rents on that home would be between $4000 and $4500 per month. At the upper end, that's an annual total of $54,000. Your rent to price ratio (divide the rent by the property value) is 5.4%.

Imagine you own the home free and clear – meaning there was no mortgage - you have $54,000 of annual rental income to cover the taxes, insurance, management and maintenance. Now imagine your one tenant moves out. You have 100% vacancy.

A million dollars invested in the mid-west will result in several homes, not just one. Imagine having 5 homes owned free-and-clear and one tenant moves out. You only have 20% vacancy. The other four properties are still producing rent. Additionally, that portfolio of homes will produce $10,000 per month in rent. That's an annual total of $120,000 produced by the million-dollar investment, which is a 12% rent to price ratio.

"Real estate investing, even on a very small scale, remains a tried-and-true means of building an individual's cash flow and wealth." – Robert Kiyosaki

Okay, crazy question here, all things being equal, you would prefer a 12% rent to price ratio rather than a 5.4% ratio, am I right? Additionally, you have the added benefit of diversification.

At this point you might be saying, 'Todd, you want me to invest in another state?!? How is that going to work? How am I going to safely invest from a distance? This goes back to Buy right and the market doesn't matter. If you buy the right inspections and the right property manager, then you can safely invest from a distance, because not only does the market direction not matter, but the specific market that you buy in also doesn't matter. It doesn't matter how far away you are from the market or if you ever actually step foot into the property. You will see it better with other's eyes, than you ever would with your own.

For example, you receive your home inspection report and it calls out an electrical issue. You aren't an electrician, so you ask your realtor for a referral to a trusted electrician and you pay him to come look at the issue and fix it. You can safely invest from a distance, if you go into it with your eyes wide open and have a

"Real estate investing, even on a very small scale, remains a tried-and-true means of building an individual's cash flow and wealth." – Robert Kiyosaki

bouncer that is only going to let the right people in. That makes sense, doesn't it?

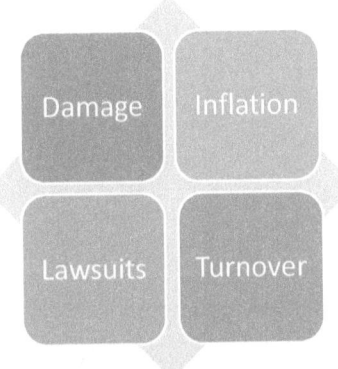

With the higher amounts of cash flow available in the midwest, let's talk about the four threats to cash flow, which are Damage, Inflation, Lawsuits, and Turnover. Now, damage can be destructive, think termites or bad tenant. It can also be disasters, such as a tornado or hail storm. This is why it is so important to have good insurance and to maintain reserve accounts for maintenance (think leaky toilets) and capital expenditures (such as replacing a roof). That is yet another reason why Cash flow is King, because you get paid upfront and don't have to provide the hamburger until Tuesday. You get the money for the repairs today and someday you do them. Make sense, right?

The second threat is Inflation of expenses without an offsetting increase in rents. A few years ago, the rates for the National Flood insurance program were raised significantly, so any rentals in those markets saw a big decrease in cash flow. This goes back to buying the right community and ensuring that you only purchase properties that produce a high cash flow. If it's raining, don't you want to be able to buy an umbrella?

The third threat to is a lawsuit. This isn't just an eviction, but can also be things like a slip and fall suit, which is why Liability insurance is so awesome. Also, a good property manager is only going to let the right people in. Agreed?

The last of the four threats to cash flow is Turnover. Not only is the paying tenant leaving, but your property now needs to be made rent ready. Your manager informs you that it has a stained carpet that doesn't show well for new tenants, but isn't really at the end of its useful life, so you decide to replace it sooner than you had planned. You pay for it with money you saved in capital expenditure account and, of course, you have money saved in your vacancy account to pay the mortgage until you have your next tenant.

All is well, because you followed the rule that Cash flow is King and you made sure to buy right.

"Real estate investing, even on a very small scale, remains a tried-and-true means of building an individual's cash flow and wealth." – Robert Kiyosaki

These four things are realities that both low cash flow and high cash flow markets face. Would you agree that the two strategies to mitigate these threats are: save for a rainy day and buy an insurance umbrella? A high cash flow property enables that, doesn't it?

We looked at the mid-west cash flow difference, how to safely invest from a distance, and how to mitigate the four threats to cash flow. That's why the place to invest is the mid-west.

"Real estate investing, even on a very small scale, remains a tried-and-true means of building an individual's cash flow and wealth." – Robert Kiyosaki

Chapter 6 –

Three Is Better Than One

"Rich people use debt to leverage investments and grow cash flows. Poor people use debt to buy things that make rich people richer."
Grant Cardone

To really bring this home for you, let's look at a case study – a deep dive on a recently purchased property.

"Real estate investing, even on a very small scale, remains a tried-and-true means of building an individual's cash flow and wealth." – Robert Kiyosaki

Let's look at a little gem on La Salle Boulevard in Warren, Michigan. It was listed at $98,500 and we purchased it with cash for $95,000 in November of 2023. Here's the notes from the Multiple Listing Service:

"Back on the market, buyer's financing fell through. This 3-bedroom 1 bath Warren bungalow occupied by a Section 8 tenant paying $1,100 per month is ready to be added to your rental portfolio! Tenant has been in the property since 2021 and is currently on a month-to-month lease. Photos are from prior to tenant move in."

At monthly rent of $1,100, that puts our rent to price ratio at 1.158%. However, since the tenant's lease had gone month to month, we were able to apply in January for a rent increase with the local housing office that manages her section-8 voucher. The 2024 section-8 rates for a 3 bedroom have risen to $1420, which is actually a bit above the open market – and it's guaranteed! That rent to price ratio is an eye-popping 1.494%!

What does that mean in terms of mailbox money? That equates to $343 per month or $4125 annually. Here's how I calculated those results: I used the section-8 rental rate and to be conservative I put in $5000 for the closing costs (we paid cash so our costs only came to $1382). Rates for a loan up to 75% of the property value at the time of this writing are around 7.5% and require a 2.0% buy-down, but considering the loan amount is so low, that's not much money; it's only $1425. Also, I budgeted 5% of rents each for vacancy, maintenance, and capital expenditures, plus 10% for property management.

With those criteria factored in, the first-year return on the cash invested, what we all "cash-on-cash return" is over 15.5%. Imagine investing $26,600 and receiving $4,125 back in spendable cash flow the first year; mailbox money. Now think about what happens to that mailbox money over the next 10 years as rents rise…assuming the long-term average of 4%, you'll receive $826 per month in 10 years; that's an annual income of $9,923…on an investment of just $26,600.

Now, the price is low enough that some of you might be thinking of buying it all in cash and not even getting a mortgage, right? Well, the advantage to the mortgage is that it increases your rate of return and will enable you to buy three of these instead of just one (and have some money left over). Let's look at those numbers. If the property was purchased with all cash, and using all of the same assumptions above, the monthly cash flow would be $842.

However, the cash flow for three of the financed properties is $1029 ($343 times 3). The interesting thing is that you end up with less cash flow by going with just one rather than three. Then there's the long-term benefit of appreciation of values and rents over the next ten years – three is better than one.

"Real estate investing, even on a very small scale, remains a tried-and-true means of building an individual's cash flow and wealth." – Robert Kiyosaki

Chapter 7

The Magic Of Ten Thirty One

"I am proud to be paying taxes in the United States. The only thing is I could be just as proud for half the money."
Arthur Godfrey

If you already own a rental in a market with a low rent-to-price ratio (like Southern California) and you like the idea of moving your investment into a significantly higher yielding market, but you don't want to pay huge capital gains taxes, then read on– this chapter is for you!

The section of the IRS code known as 1031 (pronounced "Ten Thirty-One") enables an investor to sell a rental property and avoid paying capital gains tax (or depreciation recapture tax) as long as the investor follows the rules in this portion of the tax code. The taxes are then deferred until the new property is sold (unless that sale also follows the 1031 process, enabling the investor to defer the taxes all the way until death). To be eligible

---

"Real estate investing, even on a very small scale, remains a tried-and-true means of building an individual's cash flow and wealth." – Robert Kiyosaki

for the tax deferral, there are six rules that the sale process must adhere to:

- Buy a "like-kind" property
- Buy a replacement property that is of equal or greater value than what was sold
- Reinvest all proceeds
- Have a Qualified Intermediary handle the process
- Meet the 45 day and 180-day timelines
- Use the 3-property rule, 200% rule, or 95% rule to identify what will be purchased

First is the "like-kind" rule. The investor must purchase another similar investment – the IRS term is a "like-kind exchange." This definition is fairly broad and allows just about any piece of real estate to be purchased as a replacement.

For example, a single-family house can be sold and a commercial building or vacant land can be purchased as the exchange. What cannot be purchased is something that is not real estate, such as stock certificates. Thus, investment in a Real Estate Investment Trust (REIT) does not qualify, because the investor is actually buying stock certificates and not real estate.

Second is the equal or greater value rule. The value of what the investor purchases must be equal to or exceed the value of what the investor sold. For example, if the investor sold a million-dollar home, they must buy a property or a combination of properties with total value of a million or more.

Third is the reinvestment rule. To completely defer all taxes, the investor must reinvest all proceeds. Any cash taken out of the exchange is considered taxable. However, there are ways to receive cash and I will talk about them in a few paragraphs.

Fourth is the Qualified Intermediary rule. A neutral third party, referred to as a Qualified Intermediary (QI) by the IRS and colloquially as an exchange accommodator, has to be used to hold the sale proceeds. Thus, when the sale of the relinquished property closes, the funds will be sent by the escrow company to the exchange accommodator to facilitate the 1031 exchange process. Since some sale costs can be deducted from the sale price, the QI will advise on minimum purchase price along with accounting for the sale proceeds. To me, the fact that the QI will guide the investor thru the process to ensure success, is one of the most important parts of this. That's nice to know, isn't it?

"Real estate investing, even on a very small scale, remains a tried-and-true means of building an individual's cash flow and wealth." – Robert Kiyosaki

Fifth is the timing and it has two parts. An investor has the first 45-days to identify what they will potentially purchase as their exchange. This simply means that the investor has to turn in a list of what they will buy (or have already purchased) to the accommodator before the end of the 45th day (from the sale of their relinquished property). Additionally, an investor has 180 days from the sale of the relinquished property to close on the exchange property. Also, the first 45-days are inside of this 180-days, not added to them.

Last are the identification rules. Within the first 45 days, the investor has three options for identifying potential purchases. One option is the 3-property rule, which is to identify a maximum of three properties without regard for the total combined value of the properties identified. Another option is the 200% rule, which allows the investor to identify properties that total up to 200% of the relinquished property. And the last is the 95% rule. In the event that the investor identifies more than three properties and exceeds the 200% limitation, the investor must purchase 95% of the aggregate value of the identified properties.

"Real estate investing, even on a very small scale, remains a tried-and-true means of building an individual's cash flow and wealth." – Robert Kiyosaki

Let's walk thru an example showing how significant a tax savings the 1031 exchange process can provide.

Our fictional investor purchased a home in San Diego twelve years ago at a price of $500,000. It was their primary residence for the first 5 years and has since been a rental. The market value today is a bit over $1mil. After allowable sales costs are deducted, the investor has a $500,000 gain. On that amount, the Federal Capital Gains taxes are likely to be $75,000 (possibly higher). He will also owe income tax to California of approximately $46,500. Next, we have the 20% Depreciation Recapture tax. Since the home was a rental for seven years, the investor received an annual tax deduction of approximately $18,000 for a seven-year total of $126,000. That makes the Depreciation Recapture tax over $25,200. Our tax total comes to over $146,000!! By following the 1031 exchange process the investor gets to keep that wealth.

Earlier I mentioned that there are ways that the investor can receive cash without it being subject to tax.

There are two ways to accomplish this: offsetting tax deductions or refinance after the 1031 is completed. If an investor wants to take funds out during the 1031 process and not be subject to tax, they will need to have off-setting tax deductions. Most commonly this takes the form of unused depreciation that can be applied to the funds taken out of the 1031.

In this scenario, the investor does not have to refinance the property later. If an investor doesn't have any offsetting tax deduction, then the simplest way for an investor to receive cash is to first complete the 1031 exchange process and then refinance the property to take out equity. A refinance that takes cash out of the equity and provides it to the investor does not trigger income tax or capital gains tax. Those are only triggered by the sale of the property. That makes the 1031 process an attractive option, doesn't it?

"Real estate investing, even on a very small scale, remains a tried-and-true means of building an individual's cash flow and wealth." – Robert Kiyosaki

Chapter 8

What Life Will Be Like For You

"Landlords grow rich in their sleep."
John Stuart Mill

Picture this: it's a few days into the month and, coffee in hand, you wander out to your mailbox. Mine is a slot in the side of my garage. It all dumps into a metal box. Inside the mailbox is a bit of the usual junk mail, a few bills, and the most important item

– a check from your property manager. As you stroll back into the house, you're thinking about that fact that this isn't your first check. You're a few years into this and it's been fun

---

"Real estate investing, even on a very small scale, remains a tried-and-true means of building an individual's cash flow and wealth." – Robert Kiyosaki

to receive a steady income thru your mailbox. You think, sure I've had a few repairs and things come up, but it wouldn't even be fair to call them mistakes; more like earlier than expected.

You followed the steps we've talked about. You understand what to do. You targeted high cash flow markets. You followed the criteria for buying right in order to mitigate risk, ensuring that each time you bought it was always the right time. You compounded the cash flow by reinvesting it into additional high-cash flow properties.

But today's different, because at this point you see your neighbor walking out to his car to head off to a job that he's told you time and again that he is just absolutely-over it – he hates it, but it pays well, so he keeps showing up. As watch him drive off, you set your coffee down and almost absent mindedly open the envelop. As you look at the amount of the check, the usual feelings of peace and security that you typically feel – this time they change – because this check is not only big enough to make your mortgage payment, you realize there's enough there to live off of.

"Real estate investing, even on a very small scale, remains a tried-and-true means of building an individual's cash flow and wealth." – Robert Kiyosaki

What Life Will Be Like For You

Unlike your neighbor, you now have a choice – a big choice. You can continue working if you want to, but you no longer have to you. You have time on your hands. You have freedom. That's what life will be like for you once you get the ins and the outs of our approach to finding high cash flow rental properties.

With that in mind, knowing what you now know...

Do you feel more comfortable with investing in real estate? And, can you see yourself using what I shared with you to help you grow your investments?

As far as the overall content, are you happy you read this book? Would you say your time was well spent?

If your answers are yes, then great. I'm truly glad. But here's what I know. Reading one book isn't really going to go about creating the change in your life that you want and deserve. You actually have to take action. Knowing this, as I wrote this book, I realized there were two ways to help you. The first choice is I could share what I've shared thus far and then offer to help you individually.

"Real estate investing, even on a very small scale, remains a tried-and-true means of building an individual's cash flow and wealth." – Robert Kiyosaki

If that's what you decide, great. My team and I are happy to help. But it left me wondering about the complexity and risk to you alone.

That's when I set to work on the second choice, which is that I could take a more active role and responsibility for your success, to create a situation where I would do everything I could to make your success certain...by doing it all for you. The second option is an investment pool that diversifies your risk. Instead of you buying one property alone and retaining all the responsibility and risk for that investment, I have set up what is called a real estate syndication – a group investment fund. The difference is like planning a wilderness excursion. You can work with a store like REI or Bass Pros Shops and they will sell you equipment, but you might not be properly equipped. Alternatively, you can hire a guide and they will make sure you are well provisioned, well feed, and well taken care of, because they will be living it with you. Imagine owing 5% of 20 homes rather than 100% of one.

Now at the beginning I told you that I was not going do a commercial for my team and our services, that I was going to focus on pure awesome content. And I think I have done that. I also stated that at the end I would mention this opportunity. So, if you are interested in exploring how either option can work for you, if it's exciting to you and you want to look into how to invest individually or as part of the group, visit NotSoGoldenCA.com/chat to schedule a time on my calendar to explore your options.

You're probably going to need more information to know if it's even right for you. And that's why I keep time available on my calendar every month to help you explore your options. This is a no cost, no obligation consultation. No one will apply pressure to you. I don't have a boiler room sales team. It's just me.

If you want to talk to me and you want to find out more about either option, investing individually or as part of the group, we'll have a great conversation. We'll figure out your game plan for you and at the end of it, you're going to know if this right for you or not. And if it is, what your next steps are. I will make them very clear. This is a risk-free opportunity to talk to me. All you have to do is visit www.NotSoGoldenCA.com/chat and you can schedule a time for us to chat. All you need to do to take the next step is just book the session with me.

"Real estate investing, even on a very small scale, remains a tried-and-true means of building an individual's cash flow and wealth." – Robert Kiyosaki

We are now at the end. As I wrote this book, I knew I had to walk a line between going too deep (and either creating confusion or boredom) and going too shallow (thus leaving some of your concerns unaddressed). My hope is that I nailed it just right, but I'm also a realist. So, if you have any questions, feel free to visit www.NotSoGoldenCA.com/chat schedule a time for us to chat

---

"Real estate investing, even on a very small scale, remains a tried-and-true means of building an individual's cash flow and wealth." – Robert Kiyosaki

Glossary

Appreciation: the increase in price or value of a property over time.

Cash on cash return: the ratio calculated by taking the annual profit produced by an investment (as in available to distribute to the investor) and dividing it by the total amount of cash put into the investment (such as down payment and rehab costs). For example, if an investment produces $1000 per year in cash back to the investor and it required $10,000 to purchase, it would be said to produce a 10% cash on cash return. Often abbreviated CoC.

Cash flow: the strict definition is the net balance of cash moving into (or out of) a business at a specific point in time. However, it is often used as shorthand to refer to distributable profits that an investment produces. Thus, when an investor says that a property "cash flows", they mean that the investment produces a positive cash flow sufficient to distribute profits to the investors.

Compounding: this occurs when the profit from an investment is itself invested and produces additional profits, which is the opposite of simple interest or straight-line returns. The additional profits cause far higher growth. For example, a

---

"Real estate investing, even on a very small scale, remains a tried-and-true means of building an individual's cash flow and wealth." – Robert Kiyosaki

$100,000 invested for 10 years at a simple interest of 10% would produce a total of $100,000 ($10,000 per year). The same $100,000 invested for 10 years in a compounding 10% investment would produce a total of $159,374; more than 59% higher than a simple interest investment.

Leverage: in a financial transaction refers to money borrowed and used to purchase an asset. When a rental property buyer obtains a loan, instead of buying with all cash, they are employing leverage. Since leverage magnifies gains (and losses) it is used in an effort to produce higher profits. For example, a $100,000 rental property goes up in value 5% (or $5,000). If the investor paid cash, they would have a 5% gain. However, if the investor only put down $25,000 (and obtains a loan for $75,000) then the rate of return on the down payment is 20% ($5000 divided by $25,000). Unfortunately, the reverse is also true. If the property goes down 5% in value, then the investor has a 20% loss.

Mailbox money: profits distributed to the investor by mail or electronic means (not just by the US Postal Service).

Return on equity: is the annual distributed profits that the investor received divided by the equity in the property. After the first year of ownership return on equity is a better tool to use than cash on cash return, because the

---

"Real estate investing, even on a very small scale, remains a tried-and-true means of building an individual's cash flow and wealth." – Robert Kiyosaki

original cash invested is a fixed amount whereas the equity grows over time. Thus, an investment that produces $10,000 on a $100,000 investment can be said to produce a 10% cash on cash return, but if the equity in the property now totaled $200,000, then the return on equity would only be 5%.

Rent to price ratio: is the monthly rent that a property produces divided by the purchase price (or current property value). A property that produces $1000 in rent and is purchased for $100,000 has a rent to price ratio of 1%.

Tax advantages: the tax code allows rental property to be depreciated, which means that the purchase price of the building (not the land) is treated as an expense against profits from the rental property, thus making the rental profits tax free. If there are more expenses than profits, the expense might be eligible to be applied against other income (such as from one's job).

Turnover: is the entire management process that occurs when a tenant moves out. The property must be inspected and the security deposit either used or returned. Then the property has to be made rent ready and marketed. Finally, a new tenant does a walk thru, signs a lease, and moves in. Turnover not only results in vacancy, but can result in repairs and renovations that were not planned for (or not planned for this soon).

Vacancy: a period of time when there is no tenant in the rental property and thus, no rent is being received.

Volatility: in reference to property prices refers to speed of increase (or decrease) of prices in a given a market. A market that slowly changes is said to have low volatility.

Appendix 1 – Problematic Ways Of Measuring The Success (Or Potential Success) Of A Rental Property

Cap Rate: or Capitalization Rate is a more advanced concept that takes the gross annual rent and deducts all of the operating expenses (property taxes, insurance, management, utilities, etc.). What remains is referred to as operating income and is divided by the purchase price to determine what the rate of return would be if the property was purchase all in cash (no financing). A cap rate is a way of comparing the return of a rental property against other investments, such as bonds. The reason we don't like this formula is that it doesn't tell you if the property will produce a positive or negative cashflow.

My cash flow is $X: This sounds matter of fact, but I have spoken with many an investor who thought his cash flow was a certain level only to discover that he neglected to account for some expenses; usually the unscheduled ones (vacancy, maintenance, and capital expenditures). Also, see return on equity in the Glossary.

Return on investment (or Total Return): this is more than just the cash-on-cash return, it includes any appreciation and

---

"Real estate investing, even on a very small scale, remains a tried-and-true means of building an individual's cash flow and wealth." – Robert Kiyosaki

amortization that occurred that year. If the investor is able to use the tax benefits (depreciation) to shield other income from taxation, then that tax savings would be included as well. All of that makes this a much better measure than Cash on cash return, but since it makes its evaluation against the original investment and not the current equity, it is a faulty measure.

Someone else is paying my mortgage (or my rents cover the mortgage): This is a nice feeling and is part of the dream of rental property ownership, but expressed this way, it is a vague and incomplete calculation. For example, I have heard it used to refer to situations where the rents only paid the principal and interest on the mortgage, but not the taxes and insurance. That is not a profitable rental property.

"Real estate investing, even on a very small scale, remains a tried-and-true means of building an individual's cash flow and wealth." – Robert Kiyosaki

Appendix 2 – Financing Terms For Single-Family Rental Property Loans

Cash reserves: rental property loans require the investor to have money on account that won't be used for the transaction. Depending upon the program this requirement can be equal to between two and twelve months of payments. This is often a much larger requirement than is needed on a primary residence loan.

Co-borrowers: a second person on the loan application that is not a spouse of the first person. Many programs allow this, which enables friends to pool their money together.

Co-signors (or Non-occupant Co-borrower): This is generally only allowed when the loan is being used to purchase a primary residence. It is an essential component of the Kiddie Condo strategy (see below).

Debt Service Coverage Ratio (DSCR): this loan program compares the monthly rent against the full mortgage payment (principal, interest, taxes, and insurance) to determine qualifying. The buyer's income is not disclosed.

Departing residence: the home the buyer currently lives in that they plan to keep as a rental after purchasing a new primary residence. This is often the easiest way to obtain a

---

"Real estate investing, even on a very small scale, remains a tried-and-true means of building an individual's cash flow and wealth." – Robert Kiyosaki

rental property – especially for veterans (see VA two-at-a-time below).

House Hacking: this refers to renting rooms or creating an Accessory Dwelling Unit (ADU) – think granny flat or a portion of the house (such as basement with its own entrance). We have a client, a single guy, who purchased a five-bedroom house and then rented out four of the bedrooms. He brings in $1000 more per month than his full mortgage payment.

Kiddie Condo: FHA guidelines require an owner-occupant to live in the property, but co-signors do not have to live there. Additionally, the occupant can be a full-time student with no income. Thus, Mom & Dad can buy a home with an FHA loan (3.5% down payment) for their college age "Kiddie" who will then rent rooms out. In more affordable college markets this strategy is a great way to obtain a rental with very little down payment.

Mini-dorms: this is a house near a college that has been converted to accommodate one to two college students per bedroom. Often extra rooms have been added in areas such as the garage. The goal is for the combined room rent significantly exceed what the house would otherwise rent

"Real estate investing, even on a very small scale, remains a tried-and-true means of building an individual's cash flow and wealth." – Robert Kiyosaki

Appendix 2 – Financing Terms For Single Family Rental Property Loans

for. A member of our team owns one near San Diego State – he is crushing it.

Rents can be used to qualify: for long term rentals, most underwriting guidelines allow 75% of the rents to be used to qualify for the purchase.

Short term rental: a home that is set up as a vacation rental. This makes the home a hospitality business, which requires management for check-ins & outs, bookings, and arranging a cleaning crew. It also requires full furnishings and amenities. The goal is for the combined vacation rents to significantly exceed what the house would otherwise rent for.

VA (or FHA) two-at-a-time: purchase a home using a VA loan while keeping your departing residence and the VA loan used to buy it.

VA three-peat: purchase a home with a VA loan, refinance into a conventional loan once the equity is sufficient to do so, then buy another home using your freed-up VA entitlement, repeat the cycle for a third property.

USDA and FHA 100% financing: The US Department of Agriculture offers a 100% financing program in rural areas (some of which are not as rural as one would expect, such as Ramona in San Diego County) and the FHA program can be paired with a down-payment assistant 2nd mortgage (or grant) that makes it 100% financing. Both programs require the buyer to live in the home for one year, after which the home can be rented.

"Real estate investing, even on a very small scale, remains a tried-and-true means of building an individual's cash flow and wealth." – Robert Kiyosaki

About the Authors

Todd Swanson

Todd Swanson has had a fascination with real estate investing since he was in high school, which led him to obtain his real estate license while in college. He began his real estate investment career by partnering with a buddy to purchase a triplex (one that he wishes they had held onto). Since then, Todd's focus has been on single-family homes and his experience covers everything from vacation rentals to creative financing to setting up and running a real estate investment fund.

Professionally, Todd is a California Real Estate Broker with mortgage licenses for 17 states. He assists his clients with creating real estate wealth that turbo charges their retirement income. Todd served nearly 32 years in the Marine Corps Reserve and retired as a Chief Warrant Officer 5. He lives in the San Carlos neighborhood of San Diego, CA with his wife and daughter and a really old cat, named Molly.

"Real estate investing, even on a very small scale, remains a tried-and-true means of building an individual's cash flow and wealth." – Robert Kiyosaki

Dan Williams

Dan Williams has been helping people understand the incredible power of investing in real estate for almost 20 years. Dan helps others understand how mortgage planning and management can greatly impact their wealth accumulation over their lifetime. Dan is a Certified Reverse Mortgage Professional and Certified Liability Advisor.

Dan brings his passion to helping others with real estate, mortgages, and personal finance with the same intensity as he has brought to fitness and sports over his lifetime. As a former college athlete, Dan continues to pursue fitness goals and lifestyle, including having finished 16 Ironman Triathlons.

Dan has been a Southern California resident for over 35 years and has helped almost 1000 families in his career.

"Real estate investing, even on a very small scale, remains a tried-and-true means of building an individual's cash flow and wealth." – Robert Kiyosaki

Exclusive Bonuses

Welcome to your resource haven! If you've read this far in the book, you are on a promising path to mastering the art of investing in single-family rental properties. To aid you further on this journey, we have prepared exclusive bonus content that complements the insights and strategies shared within these pages.

Here's what you get:

1. Bonus chapter – What is a Real Estate Syndication?

I like to call this Syndicate 101 – This is where we will explain what an investment Syndicate is, how it is created and then the action steps – How we got it started, how the funds are raised and getting those first few homes purchased. We will also highlight our two types of shares, why we chose those and what other features this type of investment vehicle provides.

2. Detailed Case Studies

Dive deeper with real-life scenarios that illustrate successful investment strategies in action. These case studies break down the process from property selection to tenant management, offering a clearer picture of the challenges and triumphs in the rental property landscape.

"Real estate investing, even on a very small scale, remains a tried-and-true means of building an individual's cash flow and wealth." – Robert Kiyosaki

3. Financial Analysis Templates

Gain access to customizable templates designed to simplify your financial assessments. Whether you're evaluating potential returns or setting rental prices, these tools will help streamline your calculations and enhance your decision-making process.

4. Ongoing Updates

Stay informed with regular updates on market dynamics, legislative changes, performance of previous Syndications, and investment opportunities directly relevant to single-family rental properties. Our commitment is to keep you updated, allowing you to adapt and thrive in an ever-evolving market.

How to Access Your Bonuses:

To unlock your bonuses, simply visit NotSoGoldenCA.com/bonuses.

Registration is straightforward — enter your name and email address, and you will gain immediate access to all the resources listed above.

Your Path Forward:

"Real estate investing, even on a very small scale, remains a tried-and-true means of building an individual's cash flow and wealth." – Robert Kiyosaki

Appendix 2 – Financing Terms For Single Family Rental Property Loans

As you embark on this investment journey, remember that knowledge is not just about acquisition but application. These bonuses are designed not just to educate but also to empower you to take actionable steps. With the right tools and support, your path to success in the world of single-family rentals is within reach. Invest wisely and let your journey to financial independence begin here.

Visit **NotSoGoldenCA.com/bonuses** to get your bonuses now!

"Real estate investing, even on a very small scale, remains a tried-and-true means of building an individual's cash flow and wealth." – Robert Kiyosaki

www.ingramcontent.com/pod-product-compliance
Lightning Source LLC
Chambersburg PA
CBHW031535210526
45464CB00003B/1017